WHAT DOES A Spirit-Filled Marriage LOOK LIKE?

SELECTED SCRIPTURES FROM EPHESIANS

SUSAN J. HECK

All emphases in Scripture quotations are by the author.

316Publishing.com

Original Edition, Copyright 2019
Revised Edition, Copyright 2024

Printed in Korea

28 27 26 25 24 / 1 2 3 4 5

ISBN: 978-1-63664-335-9

To Matt and Beth Turkington
whose marriage exhibits one
that is Spirit-filled.

CHAPTER 1
The Doctrines that Guide a Spirit-Filled Marriage

Selected Scriptures from Ephesians

The story is told of a mother who was reading a picture book of Cinderella to her seven-year-old daughter. As all good fairy tales end, she read, "and they lived happily ever after." This perceptive little girl sat up and exclaimed, "Oh no, they didn't. They got married!"

The Christian home ought to be a place where the lost world can look in and see Christ represented, but I am concerned that many who look into our homes today will see that the typical Christian family isn't all that different from the typical non-Christian family. Divorce rates are roughly the same; domestic abuse takes place; very little discipline of children occurs; arguing and fighting abound; and the love of the world seems to dominate in most Christian homes. The Christian family is under attack today and, as those who profess to follow the Lord Jesus Christ, we must make sure that we are living out what the Bible says regarding marriage.

When we ask ourselves the question, "What does a Spirit-filled marriage look like?", thankfully, we don't have to sort through human ideas for an answer because God has already given us the answer in Ephesians 5:21-33. Let's consider this passage as we examine God's design for a Spirit-filled marriage.

> submitting to one another in the fear of God.
>
> Wives, submit to your own husbands, as to the Lord. For the husband is head of the wife, as also Christ is head of the church; and He is the Savior of the body. Therefore, just as the church is subject to Christ, so let the wives be to their own husbands in everything.
>
> Husbands, love your wives, just as Christ also loved the church and gave Himself for her, that He might sanctify and cleanse her with the washing of water by the word, that He might present her to Himself a glorious church, not having

> spot or wrinkle or any such thing, but that she should be holy and without blemish. So husbands ought to love their own wives as their own bodies; he who loves his wife loves himself. For no one ever hated his own flesh, but nourishes and cherishes it, just as the Lord does the church. For we are members of His body, of His flesh and of His bones. "For this reason a man shall leave his father and mother and be joined to his wife, and the two shall become one flesh." This is a great mystery, but I speak concerning Christ and the church. Nevertheless let each one of you in particular so love his own wife as himself, and let the wife see that she respects her husband.

There is no way a husband and wife can live out these verses until they are first living out Ephesians chapters 1-4. It is impossible to have a Spirit-filled marriage or, for that matter, a Spirit-controlled walk, if one's own spiritual foundation isn't solid. If we don't understand the preciousness of being chosen before the foundation of the world and the joy of being adopted into the family of God; if we don't understand that Christ chose us to be holy and for good works and that this should be the norm of our lives, then indeed having a Spirit-filled marriage will be difficult. The foundation for a Spirit-filled marriage must be a core commitment to the Lordship of Christ and a commitment to follow Him in obedience in everything, including marriage. When my husband and I did premarital counseling, he often reminded the couples we are counseling that their marriage will be good if *they will walk in the Spirit*. If a couple will pursue the Lord their God with all their heart, mind, soul, and strength, and if they will not fulfill the lusts of their flesh, then they can have a marriage that honors God. We are reminded that the apostle Paul says in Galatians 5:16, "I say then: Walk in the Spirit, and you will not fulfill the lust of the flesh."

Let's look at what it means to live out Ephesians 1-4 and the foundation that must be laid if one is to have a Spirit-filled marriage. To do so, we will consider *The Doctrines that Guide a Spirit-Filled Marriage* in this chapter, and there are 13 of them, found throughout the pages of Ephesians. Then in chapters 2-5, we will consider *The Details that Grow a Spirit-Filled Marriage*, and there are four of them, found specifically in Ephesians 5:21-33. We must keep in mind that doctrine dictates duty; that is, what we believe dictates how we behave. Right thinking is necessary for right living. So, with that in mind, let's begin with the 13 details that must be in place to guide a Spirit-filled marriage.

1. Humility

A Spirit-filled marriage is first characterized by humility. As followers of the Lord Jesus Christ, you and I have been chosen by God before the foundation of the world. Consider Ephesians 1:4 (LSB), which states that "just as *He* chose us in *Him* before the foundation of the world, that we should be holy and blameless before Him in love." I encourage you to carefully consider this truth; that God would save anyone is utterly amazing and humbling! If we grasp, even to a small degree, the depth of this reality, how then can we manifest even a hint of pride in our marital relationships? There must be humility for there to be a Spirit-filled marriage.

2. Holiness

A Spirit-filled marriage is characterized by holiness. Again, consider the same verse, Ephesians 1:4 (LSB): "just as He chose us in Him before the foundation of the world, *that we would be holy and blameless before Him in love."* This is a fundamental aspect of our faith: The Lord has called us to be holy as He is holy. He did not save us to fulfill the lusts of our flesh or to have a marriage that dishonors Him. Some helpful questions to ask yourself when you reflect on the holiness of your own marriage might be: Is that how Jesus would have spoken? Is that how Jesus would have reacted? Are those the thoughts Jesus would have had in this situation? If we are to be holy, you and I must set our minds on things above and not on the things of this earth (Colossians 3:2). Holy living will result in a marriage which honors God.

3. Forgiveness

A Spirit-filled marriage is characterized by forgiveness. Why?

Because God has forgiven us of all of our sins, as Ephesians 1:7 (LSB) clearly tells us: "In Him we have redemption through His blood, *the forgiveness of our transgressions*, according to the riches of His grace." I've counseled many wives who are bitter and unforgiving toward their husbands. This is a serious and sinful attitude. I often remind these unforgiving wives that if they show no mercy they will be shown no mercy, as James 2:13 makes clear. Matthew 6:15 is equally sobering; Jesus states that if we do not forgive others, the Father will not forgive us. Dear one, we must forgive as God has forgiven us. How can we not forgive a spouse when we have been forgiven a multitude of sins? If you find that forgiveness is a problem for you, perhaps a reminder of Matthew 18:21-22 will be helpful: "Then Peter came and said to Him, "Lord, how often shall my brother sin against me and I forgive him? Up to seven times?" Jesus said to him, "I do not say to you, up to seven times, but up to seventy times seven."" Some of us are a lot like Peter; we think that seven times is a sufficient number of times to forgive someone. But Jesus says, no, how about 490 times?! I have rarely had to forgive someone for 490 offenses toward me, but I am confident that my Lord has forgiven me far more than 490 times for the exact same offense! In light of God's forgiveness of us, how can you and I be so unforgiving?

4. Generosity

A Spirit-filled marriage is characterized by generosity. Why? Because God, in His generosity, has given to us an inheritance in glory! Consider Ephesians 1:14, where Paul says of the Holy Spirit: "who is the guarantee of our inheritance until the redemption of the purchased possession, to the praise of His glory." God ordained that His Son shed His own precious blood for our sins so that we could be granted an inheritance with Him. What generosity! Many spouses are unwilling to give of their time, their energy, and their bodies to serve their spouse, but we must remember that God generously gave His Son for us and that we have a generous inheritance in Heaven. A stingy person will undoubtedly have a self-serving marriage.

5. Supernatural Living

A Spirit-filled marriage is characterized by supernatural living. A genuine child of God has indwelling power. Thought-provoking in this regard is Ephesians 1:19-20 (LSB); Paul prays that we might know "what is the surpassing greatness of *His power toward us who believe* according to the working of the might of His strength, which He worked in Christ, by raising Him from the dead and seating Him at His right hand in the heavenly places." Over the years, I have counseled many women who are living with very difficult husbands, yet you would never know that about them because their lives are filled with joy and peace. These are not qualities they muster up in their own power; rather, it is the power of the resurrected Christ living in them that enables them to rise above any difficult person or difficult situation. To be clear, this does not mean that we never confront sin in a spouse, but it does mean that we are able to speak the truth in love with respect and gentleness.

6. Peace

A Spirit-filled marriage is characterized by peace. Ephesians 2:14 reminds us that "He Himself is our peace, who has made both one, and *has broken down the middle wall of separation.*" A marriage that honors the Lord is one in which a husband and wife can sit down and rationally discuss their differences. If a couple is consistently fighting and arguing, this is a clear manifestation that they are not walking in the Spirit, but in the flesh. Before I became a believer, I had quite a temper, and often my husband would refuse to talk with me until I had calmed down. He was walking in the Spirit; I was being controlled by my flesh.

7. Prayer

A Spirit-filled marriage is characterized by prayer. Paul's prayer in Ephesians 3:14-21 (LSB) is one of the most beautiful in all of God's Word:

> For this reason *I bow my knees before the Father,* from whom

> every family in heaven and on earth is named, that He would give you, according to the riches of His glory, to be strengthened with power through His Spirit in the inner man, so that Christ may dwell in your hearts through faith; and that you, being firmly rooted and grounded in love, may be able to comprehend with all the saints what is the breadth and length and height and depth, and to know the love of Christ which surpasses knowledge, that you may be filled up to all the fullness of God.
>
> Now to Him who is able to do far more abundantly beyond all that we ask or understand, according to the power that works within us, to Him be the glory in the church and in Christ Jesus to all generations forever and ever. Amen.

Having a marriage that is characterized by prayer doesn't necessarily mean a couple has to pray together, though that is a good idea. In the early years of our marriage, my husband desired that we would pray together in bed before we dozed off to sleep. He would start first, but by the time he finished I was out for the night. Needless to say, that idea went out the window fast! Regardless of whether a couple prays together, it is imperative that both husband and wife have an active and steady prayer life. One of my mentors once challenged me by asking me who prayed for my husband and, sadly, I answered that I didn't know. She quickly admonished me to pray for him and to do it daily. That was over 30 years ago, and I am forever grateful for her admonishment. A believing husband and wife should pray not only regarding their marriage but also concerning their own (and their spouse's) personal holiness and living in light of pleasing the Lord. A Spirit-filled marriage will be a marriage filled with unceasing prayer!

8. Unity

A Spirit-filled marriage will be characterized by unity. Paul makes this clear in Ephesians 4:1-3 (LSB), when he says, "Therefore I, the prisoner in the Lord, exhort you to walk worthy of the calling with which you have been called, with all humility and gentleness, with patience, bearing with one another in love, *being diligent to keep the unity of the Spirit in the bond of peace.*" Unity is one of the most beautiful aspects not only of marriage but of the body of Christ as a whole. We don't have to fight for our own way. We can happily yield to one another. I know couples who argue about where they will eat dinner; what they will eat for dinner; what to watch on television; how to invest their monies; what type of schooling they should provide for their children; and on and on their argument list goes! We should strive for harmony rather than endeavoring to have our own way. We should joyfully give up our rights to one another. We should consider that these trivial things do not matter in light of eternity! We should do to our spouses as we would like done to us. A helpful exercise in discerning how you are doing in the area of pursuing unity would be to journal for one week how often you demand your own way in your marriage and how often you choose to yield to your spouse's desires—it might just reveal a selfish heart.

9. God-Given Grace

In addition to all these things, a Spirit-filled marriage is characterized by God-given grace. Ephesians 4:7 is clear: "But to each one of us grace was given according to the measure of Christ's gift." There is certainly much more that could be said concerning this point, but suffice to say that in this context the grace of God enables a believing spouse to exhibit love, joy, peace, patience, gentleness, meekness, and self-control. If in your marriage these qualities are not regularly being demonstrated, it may be that one or both spouses have never experienced the saving grace of God.

10. Speaking the Truth in Love

A Spirit-filled marriage is marked also by speaking the truth in love.[1] Ephesians 4:15 (LSB) reminds us that by "speaking the truth in love, we are to grow up in all aspects into Him who is the head, that is Christ." There should be absolutely no reason for a Spirit-filled couple to bite and devour each other, saying things to each

1 For a more thorough understanding of this topic, see: Susan J. Heck, *Speaking the Truth in Love in a Post-Truth World* (Irvine, Three Sixteen Publishing), 316Publishing.com.

other that aren't edifying. I would encourage you to speak truth to your spouse, making sure you are doing so at the right time and in the right place. Pray for wisdom about when to approach a sensitive subject. It is not wise to talk about difficult things in a marriage when one spouse is hungry or tired or undergoing some pressure. My husband, who was a pastor for 50 years, would often request that I not bring up controversial matters on the Lord's Day as he had the sobering responsibility of preaching the Word of God on that day. By God's grace, I endeavored to honor his request through the years.

11. Putting Off the Former Man

A Spirit-filled marriage also puts off the former man. In this regard, Ephesians 4:22-32 is a pointed passage for us all and much needed in our marriages:

> that you *put off, concerning your former conduct, the old man* which grows corrupt according to the deceitful lusts, and be renewed in the spirit of your mind, and that you put on the new man which was created according to God, in true righteousness and holiness.
>
> Therefore, putting away lying, "Let each one of you speak truth with his neighbor," for we are members of one another. "Be angry, and do not sin": do not let the sun go down on your wrath, nor give place to the devil. Let him who stole steal no longer, but rather let him labor, working with his hands what is good, that he may have something to give him who has need. Let no corrupt word proceed out of your mouth, but what is good for necessary edification, that it may impart grace to the hearers. And do not grieve the Holy Spirit of God, by whom you were sealed for the day of redemption. Let all bitterness, wrath, anger, clamor, and evil speaking be put away from you, with all malice. And be kind to one another, tenderhearted, forgiving one another, even as God in Christ forgave you.

Christian couples should be actively putting off lying, anger, stealing, corrupt speech, grieving the Spirit, bitterness, wrath, and maliciousness. Instead, they should be putting on kindness, tenderness, and forgiveness. Granted, this is a life-long pursuit, but if your marriage isn't becoming more and more a picture of Christ and the church with each passing year, then perhaps some reevaluation is in order. Both husband and wife ought to be daily saturating their minds and hearts with the Word of God. The Bible is clear that it is by hiding God's Word in our hearts that we are kept from sinning (Psalm 119:11).

12. Walking in Love

A Spirit-filled marriage is characterized by walking in love, which results in putting off all sexual sin. Ephesians 5:1-7 (LSB) reminds us:

> Therefore be imitators of God, as beloved children, and *walk in love*, just as Christ also loved us and gave Himself up for us, an offering and a sacrifice to God as a fragrant aroma.
>
> But sexual immorality or any impurity or greed must not even be named among you, as is proper among saints; nor filthiness and foolish talk, or coarse jesting, which are not fitting, but rather giving of thanks. For this you know with certainty, that no one sexually immoral or impure or greedy, who is an idolater, has an inheritance in the kingdom of Christ and God.
>
> Let no one deceive you with empty words, for because of these things the wrath of God comes upon the sons of disobedience. Therefore do not be partakers with them.

If either spouse is sinning sexually, this is not walking in love but in lust. Committing adultery is certainly not loving one's spouse, nor is it loving the person with whom one is committing adultery. Rather, when a spouse engages in sexual sins, he or she is giving into greedy lusts, resulting in sinful pleasures, which undoubtedly bring about lasting consequences (consider Proverbs 6:32-35).

13. A Man and a Woman Filled by the Holy Spirit

A Spirit-filled marriage is made up of a man and a woman who are each filled with the Spirit, which means they are controlled by the Spirit. The result of this is that they will give thanks in all things. Ephesians 5:18-20 (LSB) states, "And do not get drunk with wine, for that is dissipation, but be *filled with the Spirit*, speaking to one another in psalms and hymns and spiritual songs, singing and making melody with your heart to the Lord; always giving thanks for all things in the name of our Lord Jesus Christ to God, even the Father." Giving thanks always for all things means giving thanks both for the good times and the trying times of marriage; for financial gain and financial loss; for sickness and health; for difficult in-laws and difficult children. Christian couples need to understand that giving thanks in all things is the will of God for them, according to 1 Thessalonians 5:18.They need to rehearse to themselves and to one another that God does indeed work all things together for their good, even the difficult things.

Conclusion

If these doctrinal truths are not guiding your marriage, then, perhaps, before you get into the details that grow a Spirit-filled marriage, you should return to some fundamental, foundational principles regarding what it means to be a genuine child of God who is living by the Spirit. Self-examination in each of these areas might be a pain-staking exercise for you, but it will most certainly prove to be profitable spiritually. Ask yourself honestly if you are:

◊ Humble
◊ Holy
◊ Forgiving
◊ Generous
◊ Living by the power of the indwelling Spirit
◊ Peaceful
◊ Prayerful
◊ Walking in unity
◊ Living by the grace of God
◊ Speaking the truth in love
◊ Putting off the old man
◊ Walking in love
◊ Controlled by the Spirit
◊ Giving thanks in all things

CHAPTER 2
The Details that Grow a Spirit-Filled Marriage

Ephesians 5:21-33

Now that we've considered the doctrines that guide a Spirit-filled marriage, what then are the details that grow a Spirit-filled marriage? What does a marriage look like when both husband and wife live out what they say they believe? Paul gives us those specific details as he answers the following four questions in Ephesians 5:21-33. We will look at the first detail in this chapter and then the next three details in-depth in the following chapters.

◊ *What does a Spirit-filled person look like?* (v 21)
◊ *What does a Spirit-filled wife look like? (vv 22-24)*
◊ *What does a Spirit-filled husband look like? (vv 25-33)*
◊ *What does a Spirit-filled marriage look like? (v 33)*

What Does a Spirit-Filled Person Look Like?

> submitting to one another in the fear of God. (Ephesians 5:21)

At first glance, you might have thought, "See, the Bible says wives and husbands are to submit to each other!" But upon careful consideration, we find that this verse is really the heading to what Paul is going to address from this point in Ephesians until he reaches Ephesians 6:9, as he proceeds to deal with all kinds of household relationships. In other words, as this entire passage makes clear, we submit to one another in the fear of God in some specific ways that are directly related to our individual roles: wives are to submit by being subject to and respectful of their husbands; husbands are to submit by loving their wives; children are to submit by obeying their parents; parents are to submit by not provoking their children to wrath; servants are to submit by obeying their masters; and masters are to submit by not threatening their servants.

We submit to one another in the fear of God, the One we stand in awe of and the One to whom we will give an account for everything we've done in our bodies, good or bad, and this includes the things done in our homes and in our workplaces. I heard someone once say that when we get to Heaven, we will not be holding our spouse's hand; each of us will give account individually. If you and I are living a Spirit-filled, God-fearing life, then it will flesh itself out by obeying God in whatever He has asked us to do. Consider the passage in 1 Peter 3:1-7, where Peter lays out the responsibilities of the wife and the husband and then in verse 8 says, "Finally, all of you be of one mind, having compassion for one another; love as brothers, be tenderhearted, be courteous." Yes, we have distinctive roles and responsibilities, but we submit to one another in the sense that we obey what we are to be doing in our particular roles. What does a Spirit-filled person look like? They are submissive to whatever God asks them to do in their specific role.

If, as a spouse, you are humble, holy, forgiving, generous, living by the power of the indwelling Spirit, peaceful, prayerful, walking in unity, living by the grace of God, speaking the truth in love, putting off the old man, walking in love, being controlled by the Spirit, and giving thanks, then submission will come naturally. With that in mind, allow me to say that if you aren't clear as to what biblical manhood and womanhood are, it will be immensely helpful to you to further study those subjects. If a woman has bought into the feminist ideas of the world, then fulfilling her biblical role as a wife will be especially difficult; she must make sure that she understands both her God-given role as a woman and also her responsibility as a daughter of the King to obey the Lordship of Christ. Likewise, if a husband has bought into the idea of using the submission club to bully his wife by being harsh or threatening, he also would do well to study from the Scriptures what his God-given role is as a husband. Both husband and wife must be sitting under the shepherding of a faithful, Bible-teaching church, or the concepts of biblical manhood and womanhood will seem archaic to them.

Having seen that a Spirit-filled person is appropriately submissive in the various spheres of life, let us now turn to consider the way that submission is fleshed out in a wife's role. Verses 22-24 of Ephesians 5 explain for us what a Spirit-filled wife looks like; this is the second detail that grows a Spirit-filled marriage.

CHAPTER 3
What Does a Spirit-Filled Wife Look Like?
Ephesians 5:22

Wives, submit to your own husbands, as to the Lord.

The Greek word for *submit* means to place oneself under in an orderly fashion. We might say that the husband could be likened to a five-star general and the wife to a four-star general, or that the husband could be likened to the president and the wife to the vice-president. This word, submit, is also used in Colossians 3:18, where Paul says, "Wives, submit to your own husbands, as is fitting in the Lord." And in 1 Peter 3:1, Peter tells wives they must be submissive even to their unsaved husbands: "Wives, likewise, be submissive to your own husbands, that even if some do not obey the word, they, without a word, may be won by the conduct of their wives." This certainly does not mean that a woman is a doormat, or that she can never express an opinion or an idea. But it does mean that she willingly lets her husband make the final decisions for their family. I know this is a hard one for women, even for those who are older. The reason it is so hard is that it is a part of the curse that we inherited from our mother, Eve, and it is something that we will always fight against because of our sinful flesh. When Adam and Eve sinned, they were each cursed for their disobedience.

The woman's curse was twofold. Genesis 3:16 (LSB) says, "To the woman He said, 'I will greatly multiply your pain and conception, in pain you will bear children; your desire will be for your husband, and he will rule over you.'" God told Eve that she would have pain in childbirth and that her desire would be to rule over Adam, but that he would rule over her instead! A wife needs to understand how to let her husband "wear the pants in the family," and how to do so graciously, not giving him the silent treatment for days when she doesn't agree with him. A wife also needs to learn to make a gracious appeal when she disagrees with her husband. You might hear from a wife, "Well, if my husband loved me the way Christ loves the church, then submission would be a piece of cake." Well, maybe so, but that does not negate her responsibility. I've seen some women make important decisions without consulting their husbands; some even go so far as to purposely defy their husbands' wishes. But this is an awful indictment on the role of the wife and brings shame to the name of Christ.

The Greek word for *submit* also indicates that this is a voluntary submission, not a forced submission where the wife is beaten with the submission club by her husband. Just as the church submits to Christ voluntarily because she loves her Lord, so the wife submits to her husband voluntarily because she loves and respects him and sees submission as being for her good. Notice also that Paul says this submission is to one's own husband, not someone else's. A wife is to submit to the one with whom she has an intimate relationship, the one whom she trusts, and the one who is living out doctrinally what he believes. This submission is also done as unto the Lord; in other words, a wife submits to her own husband in order to please the Lord. When wives keep these things in mind, submission becomes a delight. I remember when I first got married, I thought that my husband and I would have a peachy keen marriage and that we would live happily ever after. In reality, rocky road—not peachy keen—described the first 10 years of our marriage. And, live happily ever after? He was lucky to live at all! I was not a submissive wife and I was certainly not going to have anyone telling me what to do. Thankfully, God saved me 10 years into our marriage, and once I started submitting to my husband, it became a joy and it was liberating! In verse 23, Paul gives us a foundational reason why wives are to be submissive to their own husbands. He says,

> For the husband is head of the wife, as also Christ is head of the church; and He is the Savior of the body.

The reason wives are to submit to their husbands is that God has ordained that the husband is the head of the wife in the same way that Christ is the head of the church. The term "head" means ruler or authority. Just as Christ leads every aspect of the body, His church, so the husband leads and directs his wife. And, as the husband keeps his wife's best interests in mind, as he makes decisions that include her, as he puts her needs before his own, then she will delight in submitting to him. What woman wouldn't? This does not mean that if your husband doesn't love you as I have described that you don't have to submit to him; you will still give an account to God for your submission or lack of it, and your husband will still give account to God for how he has or has not loved you. Paul concludes his words on the responsibility of the wife in verse 24.

> Therefore, just as the church is subject to Christ, so let the wives be to their own husbands in everything.

The church, the body of Christ, sees Christ as the head, and sees what He has said to be beneficial for her life and godliness. Just as the church submits to the commands of Christ, so also should a wife view her submission to her husband as the right thing to do, knowing that it will benefit her as she obeys the Lord. A wife's submission is a huge part of her sanctification.

Before we go on, I want to clarify that there is an exception to this command. If a husband were to ask his wife to do anything that is in direct violation to the Word of God, she would have to graciously decline and obey God over her husband. This principle is clearly set forth in Acts 5, where we read that Peter and the other apostles were forbidden to share the gospel; knowing that they were directly commanded by God to preach the gospel, the apostles responded with, "We must obey God rather than men" (Acts 5:29b, LSB). One example of this would be if a husband asked his wife to look at pornography with him. In that situation, the wife would have to decline, because she would have a biblical obligation to do so; Ephesians 5:3 (LSB) is very clear on this issue: "But sexual immorality or any impurity or greed must not even be named among you, as is proper among saints."

Another example is when an unsaved husband forbids his wife to go to church. In an effort to be respectful, a wife in that situation might tell her husband that she wants to be obedient to Hebrews 10:25 (LSB), which instructs Christians to be "not forsaking our own assembling together, as is the habit of some, but encouraging one another, and all the more as you see the day drawing near." She could make an appeal to her husband to let him choose one of several services at church that she could attend. This would still allow him to function as the head of the house and would communicate her desire to be respectful of his leadership, but it would also allow her to remain obedient to God's Word. If he continues to object to her worshiping at church, she needs to tell him she must obey God's Word. Or, in the event that a husband is abusing his wife, that wife should not submit to her husband's abuse, allowing him to go on violating the laws of God and the land, but should call on the governing authorities and the leadership of her church for help.

Wayne Grudem offers help in understanding what biblical submission is not. In his immensely helpful book, *Recovering Biblical Manhood and Womanhood*, Dr. Grudem offers the following directions to wives, clarifying what submission does not mean:

1. Submission does not mean putting the husband in the place of Christ.
2. Submission does not mean giving up independent thought.
3. Submission does not mean a wife should give up efforts to influence and guide her husband.
4. Submission does not mean a wife should give in to every demand of her husband.
5. Submission is not based on lesser intelligence or competence.
6. Submission does not mean being fearful or timid.
7. Submission is not inconsistent with equality within Christ.[2]

---

2 Taken from *Recovering Biblical Manhood and Womanhood: A Response to Evangelical Feminism*, by the Council on Biblical Manhood and Womanhood, © 2021. pp. 194-195, 208-209. Used by permission of Crossway, a publishing ministry of Good News Publishers, Wheaton, IL 60187, www.crossway.org.

A Spirit-filled wife, then, is a wife who is submissive to her own husband with a voluntary attitude, in everything, unless it violates the Word of God. Having painted for us this picture of a Spirit-filled wife, Paul goes on in Ephesians 5 to show us the responsibilities of husbands as they relate to their wives, helping us to see what a Spirit-filled husband looks like. This is the third detail regarding growing a Spirit-filled marriage.

CHAPTER 4
What Does a Spirit-Filled Husband Look Like?

Ephesians 5:25

> Husbands, love your wives, just as Christ also loved the church and gave Himself for her,

Husbands are to love their wives like Christ loved the church. This command to love uses the Greek word *agapao* which means that he is to love her even if she is undeserving of his love or is being unloving herself, and it is a love that is to be ongoing. This would be a concept foreign to the mindset of a husband in the Greco-Roman world. Men were not required to love their wives, and women were considered not much more than slaves. Wives were not permitted to go out in public without a male escort; a wife couldn't eat with a male guest in her home; a husband could divorce his wife for almost any reason, even burning his food. Jewish men would thank God daily that they were not born a Gentile, a slave, or a woman—that tells you a bit of what they thought of women. So, Christ's command here for a husband to love his wife was an astonishing thought to many a Christian man. But Christ comes along and changes even the culture! Many years ago, my husband was traveling to Burma and noted that the missionaries there would have their wives carry their books and walk behind them. He lovingly shared with them this was a cultural practice but certainly was not biblical.

I find it interesting to note that the Word of God never commands a woman to love her husband, but it does command a husband to love his wife. Titus 2 speaks of older women teaching younger women how to love their husbands, but that is the only mention of it. This doesn't mean that wives are "off the hook," though, when it comes to loving their husbands because we are all commanded to love our neighbors as ourselves—we are even commanded to love our enemies!

This is not the only place a husband is commanded to love his wife. Paul says in Colossians 3:19, "Husbands, love your wives and do not be bitter toward them." But Paul states here in Ephesians that husbands are to love their wives the way Christ loved the church. And how was that? He gave Himself for her; He humbled Himself to the point of dying for the church. When we consider this, it certainly does away with the notion that a husband can be harsh with his wife or ask her to sin. If you think about it, the husband has the more difficult and sobering responsibility—to love as Christ did. And Paul tells us in the next two verses *how Christ loved the church.* It's important for us to keep in mind that this is how Christ loved the church, because some have taken these two verses and tried to prove that these are specific responsibilities husbands have toward their wives. That is not what Paul is saying here in verses 26 and 27. Rather, he is giving us the reason why Christ gave Himself for the church.

> that He might sanctify and cleanse her with the washing of water by the word, (Ephesians 5:26)

Christ died for the church to sanctify her, which means to set her apart for Himself and for service to Him. This is certainly something that a husband cannot do for his wife. Paul also says that Christ cleanses His bride, the church, with the washing of the Word. The cleansing with the water corresponds to the baptism of the Spirit that takes place at salvation. Paul speaks of this very thing in Titus 3:5 (LSB), when he says, "He saved us, not by works which we did in righteousness, but according to His mercy, through the washing of regeneration and renewing by the Holy

Spirit." And in Hebrews 10:22 (LSB), we read, "let us draw near with a sincere heart in full assurance of faith, having our hearts sprinkled from an evil conscience and our bodies washed with pure water." I have heard some people take this verse and say that the husband is the only one who can wash his wife with the Word of God and therefore no one can teach her but him. This is a doctrinal error which prohibits women from learning from pastors and elders and from other women, as they are commanded to do in Titus 2. Paul is not saying that a wife can only learn the Word from her husband, nor is that a concept found anywhere in these verses. Paul does, however, go on to speak of Christ's glorious love for His body, the church, and His desire in salvation.

> that He might present her to Himself a glorious church, not having spot or wrinkle or any such thing, but that she should be holy and without blemish. (Ephesians 5:27)

Again, Paul is talking about the church and not about one's wife. Christ died for the church in order that He might present her as a glorious church to Himself. This means a church that is worthy of honor because she is holy and without spot or blemish. Christ wants His bride to be pure like a virgin with no spot or wrinkle, and He wants her to be holy and without blemish. Paul has already set forth this very idea in Ephesians 1:4 (LSB), "just as He chose us in Him before the foundation of the world, that we would be holy and blameless before Him in love." In fact, similar imagery is found in Revelation when it speaks of the marriage supper of the Lamb. In Revelation 19:7-8 (LSB), we read, "Let us rejoice and be glad and give the glory to Him, for the marriage of the Lamb has come and His bride has made herself ready." And it was given to her to clothe herself in fine linen, bright and clean; for the fine linen is the righteous acts of the saints."

Paul goes on to say, in verse 28,

> So husbands ought to love their own wives as their own bodies; he who loves his wife loves himself.

Just as Christ loves His own body, the church, husbands are to love their wives as they love their own bodies. Loving one's wife should be as if one is loving themself. This is certainly a tall order for the husband, but listen to Paul's logic in the next verse:

> For no one ever hated his own flesh, but nourishes and cherishes it, just as the Lord does the church. (Ephesians 5:29)

The truth is: we don't hate our bodies; we nourish them and cherish them. You love your body by feeding it, comforting it, caring for it in its entirety. You and I get up in the morning and we think about what we're going to feed our bodies and what we're going to put on our bodies. If we're cold, we get a jacket; if we're tired, we go to bed; if we're wounded, we get a bandage; if we're sick, we rest or take medicine or both; if we get dirty, we take a bath. Men don't hate their bodies and neither does the Lord hate His church. He nurtures and cares for her; in the same way, the husband should love his wife just as he loves himself. Why? Paul says,

> For we are members of His body, of His flesh and of His bones. (Ephesians 5:30)

This verse might seem a little mysterious to you at first glance, but it is simple when you stop to consider what Paul is saying. Christ watches over His church, His body, tenderly and carefully; so should the husband watch over his wife in the same way. Christ cares for us because we are members of His body, as Paul has so beautifully put forth in Ephesians in each of these verses: Ephesians 1:23; 2:16; 3:6; 4:4, 12, 16; 5:23. Christ doesn't disconnect Himself from those who are truly members of His body. We are eternally connected to Him; He does not divorce us. Therefore, the husband should also consider that he and his wife are joined as one, as the next verse states.

> "For this reason a man shall leave his father and mother and be joined to his wife, and the two shall become one flesh." (Ephesians 5:31)

This quote comes from Genesis 2:24, which says, "Therefore a man shall leave his father and mother and be joined to his wife, and they shall become one flesh." Just as the body, the church, is joined together with Christ, so a man and woman are joined together in marriage and become one flesh.

> This is a great mystery, but I speak concerning Christ and the church. (Ephesians 5:32)

The mystery of the union between Christ and the church is amazing and profound. So too is the union between a man and a woman; it also is amazing and profound. What does a Spirit-filled husband look like? He loves his wife as he loves himself by cherishing her.

In the same way that Wayne Grudem helped to clarify our understanding of a wife's submission, he also offers to us some helpful clarification regarding what a husband's leadership is not. In his directions to husbands, he writes specifically regarding what considerate leadership is not:

1. Considerate leadership does not mean harsh or domineering use of authority.
2. Considerate leadership does not imply equal sharing of leadership in the family.
3. Considerate leadership does not imply lesser importance for a wife.
4. Considerate leadership does not mean always giving in to a wife's wishes.
5. Considerate leadership is not optional for husbands.[3]

As wives, we would be wise to remember that when our husbands make decisions that we might not be comfortable with or necessarily agree with, we can rest in the providence of God. This doesn't mean we can't appeal to them or ask them to get godly counsel. But we must remember that we need to let our husbands lead, and we need to make sure we are submitting to that leader-

3 Ibid, 208-209.

ship. I have found great comfort in something Elisabeth Elliott often said, "In acceptance lies peace."

Having examined what a Spirit-filled person, a Spirit-filled wife, and a Spirit-filled husband look like, we now end with the sum of it all in verse 33 and answer the question, "What does a Spirit-filled marriage look like?" This is the fourth and final detail.

CHAPTER 5
What Does a Spirit-Filled Marriage Look Like?
Ephesians 5:33

> Nevertheless let each one of you in particular so love his own wife as himself, and let the wife see that she respects her husband.

Here's the bottom line: Husbands are to love their wives and wives are to respect their husbands. Paul says this: husbands, cherish your wives as you cherish your own body. Wives, respect, honor, and obey your husbands. On both sides, this should be demonstrated by your actions and attitudes.

I would like to detour for a moment to specifically address wives on this issue of respect, because it is sorely lacking among Christian women today. Using the acronym **RESPECT**, I'd like to offer some tips concerning the areas of a husband's life in which a wife can and should show him respect.

*Respect his **R**ole:* Your husband is your head, and as his wife, you must let him lead. Wives will attempt to control and often do, but Scripture teaches that they must allow their husbands to lead.

*Respect his **E**mployment:* Whether he is a ditch-digger or a politician, you must respect your husband's work and show an interest in it.

Respect his ***S****peech:* What this means is: listen when he speaks. As wives, we desire that our husbands listen to us when we are talking, right? In the same way, put down your phone—or whatever else you are doing—and respect what your husband has to say. Not listening to him communicates the message that you are simply not interested.

Respect his ***P****rivacy:* We all need private time. Men and women alike need alone time—time with the Lord, time to meditate, time to refresh. I know some women who think they can't do anything without their husbands and who demand that he be with them continually. As a wife, you must respect your husband's need for privacy. Respect his private thoughts, and that he may want to keep his thoughts to himself; respect that when he appears to be lost in thought, he may simply be thinking of nothing at all.

Respect his ***E****ats:* If there is one disrespectful behavior that I am grieved about (even from the early days of my own marriage), it is the wife who sees it as her job to nag her husband about what he eats or doesn't eat. We need to learn to stop trying to micromanage our husbands in this area—or any area, for that matter.

Respect his ***C****onvictions:* A woman's husband may not be on the same page as she is theologically, but she can graciously listen and reason together with him. My husband and I agree on most doctrinal issues, but on some we don't. Make it your aim to lovingly listen and to try to understand his positions.

Respect his ***T****ime:* Many women have every moment of their husband's day planned out for them. I know women who think their husbands should work all day and then come home and work all night; they expect their husbands to do the things that they, as wives, should be doing. Respect your husband's time.

My friend, these four details of how to grow a Spirit-filled marriage are the fleshing out of the doctrine that guides a godly marriage. We often rush to this passage in Ephesians 5 without considering what has been written before it. But that's like putting a Band-

Aid on a wound that is still in need of cleansing. Such a wound will get infected and, more than likely, cause further problems. A marriage whose aim is to be Spirit-filled must first have two individuals whose hearts have been cleansed by the blood of Jesus Christ and who are endeavoring to be controlled by His Spirit. Not only that, but a Spirit-filled marriage will also be growing in these areas; the wife will be submitting more today than last year, and the husband will be loving his wife more today than he did a year ago. A Spirit-filled marriage grows in these areas; it does not become stagnant, because at its foundation is the living Holy Spirit abiding in each spouse's heart.

As we draw this booklet to a close, I would ask you to examine *yourself* (not your spouse!) by asking yourself a series of questions:

◊ Is my life characterized by humility, holiness, forgiveness, generosity, living by the power of the indwelling Spirit, peace, prayer, walking in unity, living by the grace of God, speaking the truth in love, putting off the old woman, walking in love, being controlled by the Spirit, and giving thanks? Do these things describe my marriage?
◊ Am I doing my part to obey God even if my husband is not, and am I doing my part with a joyful heart?
◊ Is my submission a sign to others of my growing sanctification?
◊ Would my husband rather dwell on our rooftop than in the house with me because I am continually nagging him?
◊ Do I want my marriage to look like Christ and the church?
◊ Do I want my marriage to be an example to the lost world of Christ's love for His church?
◊ Do I want my marriage to be an example of the gospel?

Wouldn't it be great if that same seven-year-old girl who was told the story of Cinderella was looking in on *your* marriage and expressed a desire to have a marriage just like *yours* someday? Happily ever after, indeed—not just in this life, but also in the life to come!

Questions to Consider

1. (a) According to Ephesians 5:21-33, what are the responsibilities of the husband and what are the responsibilities of the wife? (b) Why is it essential, according to this text, that we carry out our God-given roles?

2. (a) What are the other responsibilities of the husband and of the wife, according to Genesis 2:18; Proverbs 19:13-14; 31:10-31; 1 Corinthians 7:1-16; Colossians 3:18-19; 1 Peter 3:1-7? (It might be helpful to make two columns, one labeled "Husband's Role" and the other labeled "Wife's Role.") (b) Write a summary sentence of what the role of the husband should be and another summary sentence of what the role of the wife should be, according to what you've learned from these passages in God's Word.

3. How does a married couple live out the fruit of the Spirit that is mentioned in Galatians 5:22-23? Give some practical examples of each of the fruits mentioned.

4. (a) How does Paul's description of Christ's sacrificial love, in Ephesians 5:25-32, help you to understand the sacrificial love that a husband should have for his wife? (b) How can a wife encourage and/or confront her believing husband regarding his need to be the husband that Christ commands him to be?

5. (a) Would you say you are a submissive wife? (Ask your husband, if you're brave enough!) (b) What things have you found to be helpful in aiding you to be submissive with a joyful attitude?

6. What are some ways that you can show respect to your husband even if he is behaving in a way that is not respectable?

7. After looking over all the roles of the wife, what is your greatest need in living out these responsibilities? Purpose in your heart to pray daily that God will help you to be a Spirit-filled wife.

Recommended reading:

◊ *The Excellent Wife*, by Martha Peace
◊ *The Exemplary Husband*, by Stuart Scott

Addendum

Not all marriages are Spirit-filled because not all spouses are Spirit-filled. If you are a woman who is married to an unbeliever, I would encourage you to study and to live out 1 Peter 3:1-6. Do not preach to or nag your husband but live out the gospel in front of him. Even a harsh, unbelieving, antagonistic husband's heart can be won by watching his wife live out her Christianity. Respect your husband, as you are commanded to by God. Respect his position, even though you may not respect his actions. Learn to be meek and quiet, as Peter commands. Meekness is not weakness; rather, it is strength under control. And quiet describes the woman who has a calm temper. Trust in God, Peter reminds us, because that is what the holy women of old did. Put your hope in God; it will enable you to submit even in the midst of difficult circumstances. Do not be afraid, and do not allow any threats your husband might make scare you out of your Christian faith. Do not violate the Word of God if your husband asks you to sin. Study, from the Scriptures, the difference between a preference and a sin.

Often, I am asked by women I counsel, "What do I do if my husband wants me to do something that makes me uncomfortable, but I'm not sure whether or not that thing is sinful?" This is a good question and one that comes up often in the counseling room.

First of all, Christian women cannot afford to avoid personal Bible reading and Bible study. A wife must be a woman of the Word. In order for a wife to know what is and is not sinful, she must know what God says is and is not sin. Often, women make issues over things that are really preferences. Every woman needs to be a woman of the Word, to be saturating her mind day and night with the Word of God, as Psalm 1 (LSB) says:

> How blessed is the man who does not walk in the
> counsel of the wicked,
> Nor stand in the way of sinners,
> Nor sit in the seat of scoffers!

> But his delight is in the law of Yahweh,
> And in His law he meditates day and night.
> And he will be like a tree firmly planted by streams of water, Which yields its fruit in its season
> And its leaf does not wither;
> And in whatever he does, he prospers.
>
> The wicked are not so,
> But they are like chaff which the wind drives away.
> Therefore the wicked will not rise in the judgment,
> Nor sinners in the congregation of the righteous.
> For Yahweh knows the way of the righteous,
> But the way of the wicked will perish.

The more we know of God's Word, the more we will know what He says is sinful and what is not. This necessitates not only daily time reading the Word, but also in-depth study of the Word, along with memorization of the Word.[4]

Secondly, a Christian wife must be a woman of prayer.[5] James 1:5 says that when we need wisdom we should ask God. If a woman is in doubt about something her husband is asking her to do, then she should pray and ask God for help and guidance. Peter says in 1 Peter 3:12 that God's ears are open to the prayers of the righteous. Jesus says that God desires to answer the prayers of His children, in Matthew 7:7-11 (LSB),

> Ask, and it will be given to you; seek, and you will find; knock, and it will be opened to you. For everyone who asks receives, and he who seeks finds, and to him who knocks it will be opened. Or what man is there among you who, when his son asks for a loaf, will give him a stone? Or if he asks for a fish, he will not give him a snake, will he? If you then, being evil, know how to give good gifts to your children, how

---

4 For a more thorough understanding of this topic, see: Susan J. Heck, *A Call to Scripture Memory* (Irvine, Three Sixteen Publishing), 316Publishing.com.

5 For a more thorough understanding of this topic, see: Susan J. Heck, *With the Master On Our Knees* (Irvine, Three Sixteen Publishing), 316Publishing.com.

> much more will your Father who is in heaven give what is good to those who ask Him!

God delights in answering the prayers of His children, but still we must ask Him.

Thirdly, there are some examination questions that might prove helpful to a wife when she is considering those things that make her uncomfortable— we might even call those things gray areas. These questions might help her decide whether such an area is sinful or not.

1. Is it something that will enslave me?
2. Is it something that will create an appetite for more?
3. Is it something that will destroy my ability to think logically?
4. Is it something that will weaken my intimacy with God?
5. Will it cause me to neglect Bible study and prayer?
6. Will it cause my body to rule over my Spirit and soul?
7. Can I ask God to bless this?

Last, but certainly not least, when a woman is unsure whether something is sinful or not, I would encourage her to seek counsel from a godly, older woman. God has provided help specifically for women in this regard, and He spells it out in Titus 2:3-5 (LSB):

> Older women likewise are to be reverent in their behavior, not malicious gossips nor enslaved to much wine, teaching what is good, so that they may instruct the young women in sensibility: to love their husbands, to love their children, to be sensible, pure, workers at home, kind, being subject to their own husbands, so that the word of God will not be slandered.

God, in His design, has commanded that older women teach younger women this sevenfold curriculum and part of it is how to love and submit to one's husband. An older and wiser woman is essential in the life of a younger woman, because so many times a young woman needs help in discerning what a sin is and what a preference is. An older woman who has age and experience is able to share wisdom and secrets of godly living with a younger woman. All women should be actively pursuing such relationships, because having someone to disciple them will save them a lot of heartache and grief in marriage.[6] If a woman is unsure whether her husband is asking her to sin or not, she should consult an older, godlier woman to give her help. In unusual cases, or where there is not a godly, older woman present, a wife could also consult her pastor or a trusted leader in her church.

Having given these four helps, I would also add that if there is something that a woman's husband has asked her to do that is not sinful but she is still uncomfortable doing, I would encourage her to appeal to her husband. She needs to communicate with him that it is uncomfortable for her and perhaps even violates her conscience. For example, perhaps a husband wants his wife to watch movies that are not enjoyable or comfortable for her; in such a situation, a loving husband should not force his wife to watch, say, a scary movie that will haunt her for days.

What should a woman do when she is asked to submit in an area that is uncomfortable for her, but she isn't sure that it is sinful? She should make sure that she's a woman of the Word and of prayer. She should ask herself some questions like the ones listed previously. And she should seek the counsel of an older, godly woman, because this is God's gracious provision for her.

---

6 For a more thorough understanding of this topic, see: Susan J. Heck, *A Call to Discipleship* (Irvine, Three Sixteen Publishing), 316Publishing.com.